WHY SHOULD I GET OFF THE SOFA?

✦ and other questions about health and exercise ✦

Louise Spilsbury

www.heinemann.co.uk/library

Visit our website to find out more information about **Heinemann Library** books.

To order:
 Phone 44 (0) 1865 888066
Send a fax to 44 (0) 1865 314091
 Visit the Heinemann Bookshop at www.heinemann.co.uk/library to browse our catalogue and order online.

First published in Great Britain by Heinemann Library, Halley Court, Jordan Hill, Oxford OX2 8EJ, part of Harcourt Education. Heinemann is a registered trademark of Harcourt Education Ltd.

© Harcourt Education Ltd 2003
First published in paperback in 2004
The moral right of the proprietor has been asserted.

Editorial: Nancy Dickmann, Jennifer Tubbs and Louise Galpine
Design: David Poole and Tokay Interactive Ltd (www.tokay.co.uk)
Illustrations: Kamae Design Ltd
Picture Research: Rebecca Sodergren and Liz Eddison
Production: Séverine Ribierre and Jonathan Smith

Originated by Ambassador Litho Ltd
Printed in China by W K T

ISBN 0 431 11091 3 (hardback)
07 06 05 04 03
10 9 8 7 6 5 4 3 2 1

ISBN 0 431 11101 4 (paperback)
08 07 06 05 04
10 9 8 7 6 5 4 3 2 1

British Library Cataloguing in Publication Data

Spilsbury, Louise
Why Should I Get off the Sofa? and other questions about health and exercise
613.7
A full catalogue record for this book is available from the British Library.

Acknowledgements

Corbis pp. **5** (Paul A Souders), **8**, **20** (Ariel Skelley), **14** (Sygma: Orban Thierry), **15** (Jim Craigmyle), **25** (Tom & Dee Ann McCarthy), **26**, **27** (Tom Stewart); Getty Images pp. **6** (Imagebank), **9**, **11** (Stone), **16**, **21** (Taxi); Photodisc pp. **18**, **19**, **24**; Robert Harding p. **4**; Sally and Richard Greenhill p. **10**; Science Photo Library p. **22**; Tudor Photography pp. **7**, **12**, **13**, **17**, **23**, **28**.

Cover photograph of boy in swimming pool, reproduced with permission of Alamy/Corbis.

The publishers would like to thank Julie Johnson for her assistance in the preparation of this book.

Every effort has been made to contact copyright holders of any material reproduced in this book. Any omissions will be rectified in subsequent printings if notice is given to the publishers.

CONTENTS

Keep a diary

Throughout the book, there are ideas for keeping a diary — a record of the exercises you do and how they help you. You can add your own notes to the diary, too.

Words appearing in the text in bold, **like this**, are explained in the Glossary.

WHY SHOULD I GET OFF THE SOFA?

If you leave a battery-operated toy switched on, buzzing gently in your bedroom, it runs down. If you leave your bicycle unused in the shed for too long, it goes rusty and the tyres go flat. If you spend too long on the sofa, you'll run down, too!

Making muscles

You have **muscles** all over your body. Some, such as those in your arms and legs, help you to move. Another kind of muscle, your **diaphragm**, helps you to breathe. Your **heart** is a special type of muscle that pumps blood around your body. When you exercise, you make your muscles stronger. This means that they can keep you going for longer and they are less likely to get damaged.

This gymnast knows how important it is to stretch and move his body! If you do not exercise your muscles, **bones** and **joints** regularly, they will not move so well and may get stiff.

Weighty matters

When you eat food, your body converts some of the **nutrients** in the food into **energy**. You need energy for everything you do, from breathing to biking. If you eat a lot and do not do much exercise, you will get more energy fuel from your food than you actually need. Your body will store the extra fuel as fat, and you will put on weight.

The feel-good factor

Getting off the sofa can make you feel good, too. If you have had a bad day at school or a row with a friend, exercise can help you to feel better. Exercise makes you feel more positive and more confident about yourself and your healthy body.

It is not just winning the cup that makes this team so happy. Exercise can make your body release **endorphins** – natural body chemicals that actually make you feel happier.

WHY IS IT BAD TO BE UNFIT?

When you are unfit your body and important body parts will not work so well and may become unhealthy. Exercising helps to keep your whole body in good working order. The most important part of your body is your **heart**, and exercise is a sure-fire way to keep your heart healthy and happy.

Have you noticed that your heart beats faster when you exercise? When you stop, you can feel it beating at top speed.

HOW DOES MY HEART WORK?

The heart is found in your chest. It is about the size of a fist. Its walls are made of solid **muscle**. This muscle contracts (tightens) the heart to squeeze blood out of it and into the **blood vessels** that carry blood around the body. Blood from the heart carries **oxygen** to your body parts, which they need to make them work.

Keep a diary

Your pulse rate is how many times your heart beats in a minute. It goes up when you exercise. The fitter you are, the quicker it returns to normal afterwards.

- Take your pulse and write it down. Take it again after running for two minutes. How long before it is back to normal?
- Exercise regularly for two weeks. Do the same test as before. Has your recovery time — and, therefore, your fitness — improved?

An easy place to take your pulse is the main **artery** in your wrist. Place the first two fingers of one hand on the inside of your other wrist, lining up with your thumb. Count how many beats you feel in 15 seconds. Then multiply this number by four. This is your pulse rate.

Why does my heart race when I exercise?

When you exercise your muscles work harder. When they work harder, they need more oxygen and **nutrients** to keep them going. You feel your heart beating faster in your chest because it is working harder, too. It is pumping more blood — which carries oxygen and nutrients to the muscles.

WHAT KIND OF EXERCISE IS BEST?

HOW DO MUSCLES WORK?

Muscles are made of hundreds of small fibres that are elastic (a bit like rubber bands). Muscles are attached to **bones** by **tendons**, which are a bit like ropes. When you contract (tighten) a muscle, the tendons move, pulling the bones with them.

The best kind of exercise is the one you enjoy most because if you like doing it you will keep going back for more! Most activities are good for you, but different kinds of exercise help you in different ways. It is best to do a variety of things to make sure that you get the three S's — strength, stamina and suppleness.

Exercise for strength

Exercise is important for keeping the **muscles** that help you move around strong. Strong muscles help you do the things you want to and keep you going longer. When you exercise regularly, you can increase the size and strength of your muscles.

Paddling a canoe is fantastic for your arm muscles – and good fun, too!

Activities such as running and bike riding are great for building strong, hard-working leg muscles. Rowing, push-ups and tennis are good for your arms. Some exercises, such as swimming, help many muscles at once.

Exercise for stamina

When your heart and **lungs** are stronger, you have more stamina – you can be active for longer without getting worn out. **Aerobic exercises** build up your **heart** and lungs. Aerobic means 'needing **oxygen**'. Aerobic exercises, such as swimming, running, football, dancing and cycling, make you breathe hard to get the extra oxygen your muscles need to

When you swim, you breathe harder, and that gives your heart and lungs some well-needed exercise.

keep going. This gives your lungs and heart a workout, too – your lungs breathe deeply and more quickly, and your heart pumps faster to send more oxygen in the blood to your muscles.

WHY SHOULD I CARE ABOUT MY JOINTS?

Without joints, you would not be able to move! Joints are where your bones meet, and they allow your bones to move. You have joints at your elbows, knees, ankles, shoulders and many other parts.

Exercise for suppleness

Being supple means that your body is flexible – it can stretch and bend easily. Most young people are naturally supple – they can touch their toes, and bend and roll without much trouble. As people get older, they often become less supple. This is because their **joints** become stiffer and their **muscles** become weaker – usually because they do not get enough exercise.

To keep your body supple, try doing activities such as dancing, gymnastics and martial arts, where you have to bend and stretch your body.

You do not need to become a gymnast to get supple! Just try some easy indoor exercises, such as gentle stretching and bending, to keep yourself flexible.

It does not matter whether your team wins or loses a match. The important thing about team games is exercising, enjoying yourself and making friends.

What is so good about team sports?

Football, netball, hockey, rugby, volleyball – the list of team games seems endless. What is so good about them? When you play for a team, you do much more than build up your strength, stamina and suppleness. Cooperating with team mates is a good lesson in working with others and a great way to make new friends, as you share the team's excitement, successes and disappointments.

Keep a diary

- In your diary, keep a record of what kinds of exercise you do each day for two weeks.

- Note whether you think it helped your strength, stamina or suppleness. (Some activities – such as swimming – do all three!)

- Which kind of exercise do you do most? Which do you enjoy most?

11

WHY SHOULD I DO WARM-UPS?

Muscles and tendons are pretty strong, but if you suddenly start pulling and twisting them before they have been warmed up, you can hurt them. The pain usually only lasts a little while, but it is a risk you do not have to take if you spend some time doing warm-up exercises first.

Preparing for action!

Doing warm-ups raises the temperature of the cells in your body, which increases their activity rate. Warm-ups also increase the supply of blood to the muscles, which brings more oxygen and nutrients to give them energy. They also release fluids around the joints in your body so that they move more smoothly.

Warm-ups reduce the chances of muscle strain – when you tear some of the tiny muscle fibres, leaving your muscle sore and tender. Warm-ups make your muscles and tendons more elastic and flexible.

Which warm-ups are best?

The best kinds of warm-ups start off fairly gently, such as brisk walking or slow jogging to get your blood circulating. If you are jogging on the spot, change direction often. Then try stretching different parts of your body to loosen up the joints and warm up the muscles. Slowly stretch a body part, such as an arm or leg, and hold that stretch for 20 seconds. (Never stretch so far that it hurts and never bounce while stretching.) Finally, do something a bit more energetic, such as a short, fast run, to get you out of breath and ready for action.

Toe touches, like this, are a good stretching exercise. Stand straight with your feet slightly apart and arms stretched out to the sides. Twist your body (keeping your arms straight), and touch your left toes with your right hand, and then your right toes with your left hand.

WHY DO COOL-DOWNS AFTER EXERCISE?

Exercise can make you hot and, if you stop suddenly, you can get very cold – and even catch a chill. Cool-downs help you cool down gradually and safely.

When you see a winning athlete jogging gently around the track, they are not just enjoying their moment of glory. Gentle jogging is also a form of cooling down – a way of making sure that the body winds down properly after exercise.

Slowing down!

Cool-downs allow your body temperature, breathing and **heart** rate to return to normal gradually. It is especially important to let your heart beat get back to its regular rate for it to function properly. If you stop exercise suddenly, blood in your body may stay around your leg **muscles**, instead of returning to the heart and brain. This can make you feel light-headed or dizzy.

Cool-downs also help the rest of your body get back to normal slowly, rather than suddenly. Flopping into a chair straight after exertion can make your muscles ache. Cool-downs help your muscles to loosen up again gradually after they have tightened during exercise.

Which cool-downs should I do?

The idea of cool-downs is to let your body slow down by keeping slightly active, say with a brisk walk or gentle jogging. Try to gently stretch all your muscles, particularly those you used most for the exercise. Shake your arms and legs loosely. Bend your neck and back. You can do the same kind of stretching exercises that you use for warm-ups. You should spend about five minutes on your cool-downs.

Cool-downs do not have to be complicated. Taking five minutes to walk and talk with a friend is an ideal cool-down.

HOW OFTEN SHOULD I EXERCISE?

By doing a chore like cleaning the car, you will not only get fitter – you will also earn some major Brownie points with your family.

You should really aim to do some kind of **aerobic exercise** at least two to three times a week for 20 to 30 minutes at a time. When you think that this includes games lessons at school and the break times you spend playing football, it is not all that much, really. Even dancing and playing hopscotch are aerobic activities.

Find the time

If you have trouble making time for exercise, fit it into your schedule in other ways, perhaps by walking or cycling to school instead of getting a lift. Walk up the stairs instead of using escalators or lifts. Help out with some household chores such as vacuuming the carpets or digging in the garden.

Can I do too much exercise?

Some people say that you cannot have too much of a good thing. With exercise, you can. If you suddenly start running long distances or playing football all day, you may end up in pain. Feeling weak, dizzy or sick may also be signs that you have done too much. Exercise gradually, building up the amount you do each week, until your body is ready to do more. Do not overdo the amount of exercise you do – just make it a regular part of your life.

Keep a diary

- Keep a record of the amount of exercise you do every week for the six weeks of your diary. Include the time it takes to walk to school and, if you play chase, skipping or football at break time, include that, too.
- How much exercise did you do in a week?

Do not worry about how much distance you cover when you exercise – the important thing is to enjoy it.

WHY SHOULD I WEAR TRAINERS?

Why does it matter what we wear when we exercise? The right gear allows you to move easily, and can protect your body from bumps.

The right stuff

For most sports, shorts, a T-shirt and a pair of trainers are all you need, but some sports require special gear. For example, leotards and swimming costumes are extra stretchy, so they are easy to move in.

When you run, your feet hit the ground hard. Trainers have padded soles that absorb the shock, so that your feet do not have to.

You also need to make sure that you wear the right footwear for the exercise you do. Football boots have studs in the bottom to grip on the ground, and tennis shoes are shaped to support the arch of your feet and your ankles as you twist and spin on the court.

Protecting your body

If you play a sport where there is a risk of your eyes getting hit by an object such as a ball, you should wear some form of eye protection, for example goggles or a guard that fits to a helmet. Squash players usually wear protective goggles to shield their eyes from fast-flying balls, and ice hockey players wear helmets to protect their eyes and rest of their head.

Wearing the right protective gear is not just for beginners. The world's top swimmers wear goggles when they race.

Helmets and pads

Your head houses a very important part of the body – the brain. Your skull does its best to protect the brain but, if you do sports where there is a risk of falling on or bumping your head, you need a helmet. You should, for example, wear a helmet while riding a bike, a horse or a scooter, and when you go rollerblading or skateboarding.

You can wear pads to protect other parts of your body when biking, skating or playing sports such as football, rugby and hockey. Pads are like cushions that you strap tightly to elbows, shins and knees. They protect your skin and the **bones**, **joints** and **muscles** beneath the skin from being broken or bruised.

When choosing a bicycle helmet, make sure you get one that is the right size, so that it does not slide about. Always wear it straight, not tilted back.

SHOULD I EAT SPECIAL FOOD?

Adverts often show athletes tucking into special food and drinks, trying to convince you that they can make you fitter and faster. In fact, all you need to do is to eat the right amount of a variety of foods, to keep fuelled-up for fun.

Bananas are a good energy snack, but do not eat anything less than one hour before a match, because it might make you feel sick.

Food for fitness

To be healthy, we all need to eat the right balance of the four different types of food – **carbohydrates**, fruit and vegetables, **proteins** and fatty or sugary foods. Carbohydrates, such as pasta and bread, give you **energy**. Try to eat one of these at every meal. Fruit and vegetables are excellent sources of **vitamins**, which help you to grow and protect you from illness. Try to eat at least five different kinds every day.

21

You need **protein**-rich foods, such as meat, fish, eggs, milk and beans, to grow strong and keep well, but you only need small amounts. Your body needs small amounts of fatty foods, such as oil or butter, to give you **energy** and to help your body **cells** to form properly.

Water works

You need to drink water every day, but you always need more when you exercise. When you are active, especially in hot weather, you **sweat**. Your body cools itself by releasing water through the **sweat glands** in your skin. If you do not replace the water you lose, you get **dehydrated**. This does not just mean that you feel really thirsty. Your body needs water to work properly and, if you get dehydrated, you may feel dizzy, weak or sick, too.

Dehydration is dangerous, so always pack a bottle of water in your kit bag, along with your shorts and trainers!

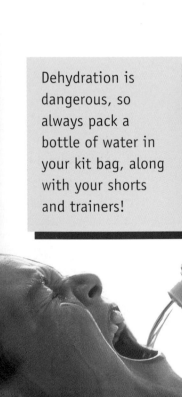

WHY DOES EXERCISE HURT SOMETIMES?

Our bodies use pain to tell us things. When exercise hurts, it is your body's way of telling you that something is wrong! If you feel pain when you exercise, you should stop immediately and get it checked out.

Stitch and cramp

Some pains, such as stitch and cramp, hit you suddenly, but are not really serious. Stitch is a sharp, stabbing pain in your side that people often get when they run soon after eating. **Oxygen** goes to the busy leg **muscles**, and the stomach muscles do not get enough to **digest** the food, so they hurt. Cramp is when a muscle suddenly starts tightening by itself. It can happen when you work a particular muscle too hard.

Muscles may ache after exercise if you have not done any for a while. This is not necessarily bad pain. Rubbing and gently stretching should make the muscles feel better.

Serious damage?

Sometimes a pain is more serious, such as a broken **bone** or a damaged **muscle**. When you have a pain that does not go away completely after a few minutes, ask an adult to look at it. You should also ask for help if you feel dizzy or sick, or have a headache.

Getting breathless

You breathe faster when you exercise, because your body needs to get extra **oxygen** to your muscles. Remember to breathe properly during exercise – always breathe in through your nose and out through your mouth, and never hold your breath. If you start panting and feel really out of breath, take a break. If you exercise too hard or fast, you may end up feeling dizzy or sick.

Do not let the risk of getting hurt put you off – few people your age get hurt doing exercise. In fact, you are more likely to have health problems if you do not exercise.

PAIN PREVENTION

Here are some top tips for things that you can do to avoid being hurt when you exercise.

- Do not play a game or do a sport that you are not strong or fit enough to do.

- Always follow the rules of the game and encourage the other members of your team to do the same.

- Wear and use the right gear and equipment for the right sports.

- Always warm-up before exercise and cool-down properly afterwards.

- Never play when you are tired or in any pain.

  - Wear sun cream and a hat to prevent sunburn, and drink lots of water to prevent **dehydration**, if you play games outside on hot days.

Rules are made to keep you safe. A careless push in basketball could cause injuries. Referees are there to make sure that both teams follow the rules.

WHAT IF I DO NOT LIKE TEAM SPORTS?

Have you ever jumped on a bouncy castle, flown a kite or walked the dog? If so, you have been getting good exercise without having to join a team or attend practice sessions. Lots of people enjoy team games, but there are many other ways of keeping fit.

Keep fit with a friend

Mark out a hopscotch grid with chalk, and play with friends.

When a friend comes home to play, why not take the chance to exercise? Play badminton or tennis, or have running races in the garden or the park. Play frisbee or catch with a soft ball. Work out a dance routine together or play chase. You do not have to be in a team to enjoy team games – why not mark out a goal, and practice shooting and goal-keeping skills, or get a rounders bat and throw some balls to each other?

Spinning a hula hoop is a great exercise to do alone. See how many spins you can do before it falls!

Keep fit alone

There are lots of ways to exercise on your own. Go for a bike ride, set up a slalom course to zig-zag in and out of on your roller blades, or see how many jumps you can do with a skipping rope. Set up a basket and practise scoring hoops, or hit a tennis ball against a wall and improve your backhand.

PLAY IT SAFE

If you exercise outside, alone or with a friend, play it safe.

- Tell an adult where you are going.
- Keep away from traffic. Do not kick balls near a road – you could put yourself and others in danger.
- Never talk to strangers.
- Always go home when you said you would.

WHAT IF IT IS RAINING OUTSIDE?

Just because it is raining outside, it does not mean that you should flop back onto the sofa. There are plenty of things you can do indoors. Turn on some music and dance. Hop on one foot or jog on the spot. Try some star jumps or stretches. Practise some rolls and other gymnastic moves along the hall.

Why not blow up a balloon and play volleyball, or keep hitting it to keep it off the floor?

Sports centres

You will also find lots of indoor exercise ideas at your local sports centre. When autumn starts, sign up for a new class in swimming, judo, trampoline, badminton or indoor tennis. Or take up indoor roller-skating, ice-skating or even indoor bowling. Whatever you choose to do – have fun and keep fit!

EXERCISE INFORMATION

Before doing exercise or playing a match, don't forget to do your warm-ups and cool-downs. In these two sets of pictures, the children are doing gentle stretches to warm-up before exercise, and some brisk walking to cool-down after exercise.

GLOSSARY

aerobic exercise   exercise that makes you breathe harder. Aerobic means 'needing oxygen'.

arteries   blood vessels that carry blood from the heart to other parts of the body

blood vessels   tubes carrying blood round the body

bones   solid body parts that fit together to form the skeleton that supports the soft parts of your body

carbohydrates   kind of food that gives you energy

cells   smallest building block of living things

dehydrated   when your body loses more water, for example by sweating, than you take in

diaphragm   muscle between the ribs and stomach

digest   to break down the food we eat into nutrients to give us energy

endorphins   natural chemicals in the body that are released into your system when you exercise

energy   energy allows living things to do everything they need to live and grow

heart   body part that pumps blood through the blood vessels

joint   place where two bones inside your body join

lungs   body parts that breathe in air and take in oxygen

muscles   parts of your body that pull on the bones to make them move

nutrients   kinds of chemicals found in food that our bodies need to stay healthy

oxygen   gas in the air that we breathe in to live

proteins   substances in some of the foods we eat that our bodies can use to build or repair body parts

sweat   salty water that your body releases through your skin

sweat glands   parts of the body that sweat

tendons   fibres that attach bones to muscles

vitamins   substances found in food that are vital to your health

FURTHER READING

Why Do Bones Break? And Other Questions About Movement, Angela Royston (Heinemann Library, 2002)

Why Do Bruises Change Colour? And Other Questions About Blood, Angela Royston (Heinemann Library, 2002)

INDEX